'But I ran broken stairway, and came out suddenly, as by a miracle, clean on the platform of my San Tommaso, in the tremendous sunshine.'

D. H. LAWRENCE
Born 1885, Eastwood, England
Died 1930, Vence, France

'The Spinner and the Monks', 'Il Duro' and 'John' are taken
from *Twilight in Italy*, first published in 1916.
'The Florence Museum' is taken from *Etruscan Places*,
first published in 1932.

D. H. LAWRENCE

Il Duro

PENGUIN BOOKS

PENGUIN CLASSICS

UK | USA | Canada | Ireland | Australia
India | New Zealand | South Africa

Penguin Books is part of the Penguin Random House group of companies
whose addresses can be found at global.penguinrandomhouse.com.

This selection published in Penguin Classics 2015
002

Set in 9.5/13 pt Baskerville 10 Pro
Typeset by Jouve (UK), Milton Keynes
Printed in Great Britain by Clays Ltd, St Ives plc

A CIP catalogue record for this book is available from the British Library

ISBN: 978-0-141-39863-1

www.greenpenguin.co.uk

Contents

The Spinner and the Monks

The Holy Spirit is a Dove, or an Eagle. In the Old Testament it was an Eagle; in the New Testament it is a Dove.

And there are, standing over the Christian world, the Churches of the Dove and the Churches of the Eagle. There are, moreover, the Churches which do not belong to the Holy Spirit at all, but which are built to pure fancy and logic; such as the Wren Churches in London.

The Churches of the Dove are shy and hidden: they nestle among trees, and their bells sound in the mellowness of Sunday; or they are gathered into a silence of their own in the very midst of the town, so that one passes them by without observing them; they are as if invisible, offering no resistance to the storming of the traffic.

But the Churches of the Eagle stand high, with their heads to the skies, as if they challenged the world below. They are the Churches of the Spirit of David, and their bells ring passionately, imperiously, falling on the subservient world below.

The Church of San Francesco was a Church of the Dove. I passed it several times, in the dark, silent little square, without knowing it was a church. Its pink walls were blind, windowless, unnoticeable, it gave no sign, unless one caught sight of the tan curtain hanging in the door, and the slit of darkness beneath. Yet it was the chief church of the village.

But the Church of San Tommaso perched over the village. Coming down the cobbled, submerged street, many a time I looked up between the houses and saw the thin old church standing above in the light, as if it perched on the house-roofs. Its thin grey neck was held up stiffly, beyond was a vision of dark foliage, and the high hillside.

I saw it often, and yet for a long time it never occurred to me that it actually existed. It was like a vision, a thing one does not expect to come close to. It was there standing away upon the house-tops, against a glamour of foliaged hillside. I was submerged in the village, on the uneven, cobbled street, between old high walls and cavernous shops and the houses with flights of steps.

For a long time I knew how the day went, by the imperious clangour of midday and evening bells striking down upon the houses and the edge of the lake. Yet it did not occur to me to ask where these bells rang. Till at last my everyday trance was broken in upon, and I knew the ringing of the Church of San Tommaso. The church became a living connection with me.

So I set out to find it, I wanted to go to it. It was very near. I could see it from the piazza by the lake. And the village itself had only a few hundreds of inhabitants. The church must be within a stone's throw.

Yet I could not find it. I went out of the back door of the house, into the narrow gulley of the back street. Women glanced down at me from the top of the flights of steps, old men stood, half-turning, half-crouching under the dark shadow of the walls, to stare. It was as if the strange creatures of the under-shadow were looking at me. I was of another element.

The Italian people are called 'Children of the Sun.' They might better be called 'Children of the Shadow.' Their souls are dark and nocturnal. If they are to be easy, they must be able to hide, to be hidden in lairs and caves of darkness. Going through these tiny, chaotic back-ways of the village was like venturing through the labyrinth made by furtive creatures, who watched from out of another element. And I was pale, and clear, and evanescent, like the light, and they were dark, and close, and constant, like the shadow.

So I was quite baffled by the tortuous, tiny, deep passages of the village. I could not find my way. I hurried towards the broken end of a street, where the sunshine and the olive trees looked like a mirage before me. And there above me I saw the thin, stiff neck of old San Tommaso, grey and pale in the sun. Yet I could not get up to the church, I found myself again on the piazza.

Another day, however, I found a broken staircase, where weeds grew in the gaps the steps had made in falling, and maidenhair hung on the darker side of the wall. I went up unwillingly, because the Italians used this old staircase as a privy, as they will any deep side-passage.

But I ran up the broken stairway, and came out suddenly, as by a miracle, clean on the platform of my San Tommaso, in the tremendous sunshine.

It was another world, the world of the eagle, the world of fierce abstraction. It was all clear, overwhelming sunshine, a platform hung in the light. Just below were the confused, tiled roofs of the village, and beyond them the pale blue water, down below; and opposite, opposite my face and breast, the clear, luminous snow of the mountain across the lake, level with me apparently, though really much above.

I was in the skies now, looking down from my square terrace of cobbled pavement, that was worn like the threshold of the ancient church. Round the terrace ran a low, broad wall, the coping of the upper heaven where I had climbed.

There was a blood-red sail like a butterfly breathing down on the blue water, whilst the earth on the near side gave off a green-silver smoke of olive trees, coming up and around the earth-coloured roofs.

It always remains to me that San Tommaso and its terrace hang suspended above the village, like the lowest step of heaven, of Jacob's ladder. Behind, the land rises in a high sweep. But the terrace of San Tommaso is let down from heaven, and does not touch the earth.

I went into the church. It was very dark, and impregnated with centuries of incense. It affected me like the lair of some enormous creature. My senses were roused, they sprang awake in the hot, spiced darkness. My skin was expectant, as if it expected some contact, some embrace, as if it were aware of the contiguity of the physical world, the physical contact with the darkness and the heavy, suggestive substance of the enclosure. It was a thick, fierce darkness of the senses. But my soul shrank.

I went out again. The pavemented threshold was clear as a jewel, the marvellous clarity of sunshine that becomes blue in the height seemed to distil me into itself.

Across, the heavy mountain crouched along the side of the lake, the upper half brilliantly white, belonging to the sky, the lower half dark and grim. So then, that is where heaven and earth are divided. From behind me, on the left, the headland swept down out of a great, pale-grey, arid height, through a rush of russet and crimson, to the olive smoke and the water of the level earth. And between, like a blade of the sky cleaving the earth asunder, went the pale-blue lake, cleaving mountain from mountain with the triumph of the sky.

Then I noticed that a big, blue-checked cloth was spread on the parapet before me, over the parapet of heaven. I wondered why it hung there.

Turning round, on the other side of the terrace, under a caper-bush that hung like a blood-stain from the grey wall above her, stood a little grey woman whose fingers

5

were busy. Like the grey church, she made me feel as if I were not in existence. I was wandering by the parapet of heaven, looking down. But she stood back against the solid wall, under the caper-bush, unobserved and unobserving. She was like a fragment of earth, she was a living stone of the terrace, sun-bleached. She took no notice of me, who was hesitating looking down at the earth beneath. She stood back under the sun-bleached solid wall, like a stone rolled down and stayed in a crevice.

Her head was tied in a dark-red kerchief, but pieces of hair, like dirty snow, quite short, stuck out over her ears. And she was spinning. I wondered so much, that I could not cross towards her. She was grey, and her apron, and her dress, and her kerchief, and her hands and her face were all sun-bleached and sun-stained, greyey, bluey, browny, like stones and half-coloured leaves, sunny in their colourlessness. In my black coat, I felt myself wrong, false, an outsider.

She was spinning, spontaneously, like a little wind. Under her arm she held a distaff of dark, ripe wood, just a straight stick with a clutch at the end, like a grasp of brown fingers full of a fluff of blackish, rusty fleece, held up near her shoulder. And her fingers were plucking spontaneously at the strands of wool drawn down from it. And hanging near her feet, spinning round upon a black thread, spinning busily, like a thing in a gay wind, was her shuttle, her bobbin wound fat with the coarse, blackish worsted she was making.

All the time, like motion without thought her fingers teased out the fleece, drawing it down to a fairly uniform thickness: brown, old, natural fingers that worked as in a sleep, the thumb having a long grey nail; and from moment to moment there was a quick, downward rub, between thumb and forefinger, of the thread that hung in front of her apron, the heavy bobbin spun more briskly, and she felt again at the fleece as she drew it down, and she gave a twist to the thread that issued, and the bobbin spun swiftly.

Her eyes were clear as the sky, blue, empyrean, transcendent. They were clear, but they had no looking in them. Her face was like a sun-worn stone.

'You are spinning,' I said to her.

Her eyes glanced over me, making no effort of attention.

'Yes,' she said.

She saw merely a man's figure, a stranger, standing near. I was a bit of the outside, negligible. She remained as she was, clear and sustained like an old stone upon the hillside. She stood short and sturdy, looking for the most part straight in front, unseeing, but glancing from time to time, with a little, unconscious attention, at the thread. She was slightly more animated than the sunshine and the stone and the motionless caper-bush above her. Still her fingers went along the strand of fleece near her breast.

'That is an old way of spinning,' I said.

'What?'

She looked up at me with eyes clear and transcendent as the heavens. But she was slightly roused. There was the slight motion of the eagle in her turning to look at me, a faint gleam of rapt light in her eyes. It was my unaccustomed Italian.

'That is an old way of spinning,' I repeated.

'Yes – an old way,' she repeated, as if to say the words so that they should be natural to her. And I became to her merely a transient circumstance, a man, part of the surroundings. We divided the gift of speech, that was all.

She glanced at me again, with her wonderful, unchanging eyes, that were like the visible heavens, unthinking, or like two flowers that are open in pure clear unconsciousness. To her I was a piece of the environment. That was all. Her world was clear and absolute, without consciousness of self. She was not self-conscious, because she was not aware that there was anything in the universe except *her* universe. In her universe I was a stranger, a foreign *signore*. That I had a world of my own, other than her own, was not conceived by her. She did not care.

So we conceive the stars. We are told that they are other worlds. But the stars are the clustered and single gleaming lights in the night-sky of our world. When I come home at night, there are the stars. When I cease to exist as the microcosm, when I begin to think of the cosmos, then the stars are other worlds. Then the macrocosm absorbs me. But the macrocosm is not me. It is something which I, the microcosm, am not.

So that there is something which is unknown to me and which nevertheless exists. I am finite, and my understanding has limits. The universe is bigger than I shall ever see, in mind or spirit. There is that which is not me.

If I say 'The planet Mars is inhabited,' I do not know what I mean by 'inhabited,' with reference to the planet Mars. I can only mean that that world is not my world. I can only know there is that which is not me. I am the microcosm, but the macrocosm is that also which I am not.

The old woman on the terrace in the sun did not know this. She was herself the core and centre to the world, the sun, and the single firmament. She knew that I was an inhabitant of lands which she had never seen: But what of that! There were parts of her own body which she had never seen, which physiologically she could never see. They were none the less her own because she had never seen them. The lands she had not seen were corporate parts of her own living body, the knowledge she had not attained was only the hidden knowledge of her own self. She *was* the substance of the knowledge, whether she had the knowledge in her mind or not. There was nothing which was not herself, ultimately. Even the man, the male, was part of herself. He was the mobile, separate part, but he was none the less herself because he was sometimes severed from her. If every apple in the world were cut in two, the apple would not be changed. The reality is the apple, which is just the same in the half apple as in the whole.

And she; the old spinning-woman, was the apple, eternal, unchangeable, whole even in her partiality. It was this which gave the wonderful clear unconsciousness to her eyes. How could she be conscious of herself, when all was herself?

She was talking to me of a sheep that had died, but I could not understand, because of her dialect. It never occurred to her that I could not understand. She only thought me different, stupid. And she talked on. The ewes had lived under the house, and a part was divided off for the he-goat, because the other people brought their she-goats to be covered by the he-goat. But how the ewe came to die I could not make out.

Her fingers worked away all the time in a little, half-fretful movement, yet spontaneous as butterflies leaping here and there. She chattered rapidly on in her Italian that I could not understand, looking meanwhile into my face, because the story roused her somewhat. Yet not a feature moved. Her eyes remained candid and open and unconscious as the skies. Only a sharp will in them now and then seemed to gleam at me, as if to dominate me.

Her shuttle had caught in a dead chicory plant, and spun no more. She did not notice. I stooped and broke

off the twigs. There was a glint of blue on them yet. See-
ing what I was doing, she merely withdrew a few inches
from the plant. Her bobbin hung free.

She went on with her tale, looking at me wonderfully.
She seemed like the Creation, like the beginning of the
world, the first morning. Her eyes were like the first morning of the world, so ageless.

Her thread broke. She seemed to take no notice, but
mechanically picked up the shuttle, wound up a length
of worsted, connected the ends from her wool strand, set
the bobbin spinning again, and went on talking, in her
half-intimate, half-unconscious fashion, as if she were
talking to her own world in me.

So she stood in the sunshine on the little platform, old
and yet like the morning, erect and solitary, sun-coloured,
sun-discoloured, whilst I at her elbow, like a piece of
night and moonshine, stood smiling into her eyes, afraid
lest she should deny me existence.

Which she did. She had stopped talking, did not look
at me any more, but went on with her spinning, the brown
shuttle twisting gaily. So she stood, belonging to the sunshine and the weather, taking no more notice of me than
of the dark-stained caper-bush which hung from the wall
above her head, whilst I, waiting at her side, was like the
moon in the daytime sky, over-shone, obliterated, in spite
of my black clothes.

'How long has it taken you to do that much?' I asked.

She waited a minute, glanced at her bobbin.

'This much? I don't know. A day or two.'

'But you do it quickly.'

She looked at me, as if suspiciously and derisively. Then, quite suddenly, she started forward and went across the terrace to the great blue-and-white checked cloth that was drying on the wall. I hesitated. She had cut off her consciousness from me. So I turned and ran away, taking the steps two at a time, to get away from her. In a moment I was between the walls, climbing upwards, hidden.

The school-mistress had told me I should find snow-drops behind San Tommaso. If she had not asserted such confident knowledge I should have doubted her translation of *perce-neige*. She meant Christmas roses all the while.

However, I went looking for snowdrops. The walls broke down suddenly, and I was out in a grassy olive orchard, following a track beside pieces of fallen over-grown masonry. So I came to skirt the brink of a steep little gorge, at the bottom of which a stream was rushing down its steep slant to the lake. Here I stood to look for my snowdrops. The grassy, rocky bank went down steep from my feet. I heard water tittle-tattling away in deep shadow below. There were pale flecks in the dimness, but these, I knew, were primroses. So I scrambled down.

Looking up, out of the heavy shadow that lay in the cleft, I could see, right in the sky, grey rocks shining transcendent in the pure empyrean. 'Are they so far up?' I thought. I did not dare to say, 'Am I so far down?' But I was uneasy. Nevertheless it was a lovely place, in the cold shadow, complete; when one forgot the shining rocks far above, it was a complete, shadowless world of shadow. Primroses were everywhere in nests of pale bloom upon the dark, steep face of the cleft, and tongues of fern hanging out, and here and there under the rods and twigs of bushes were tufts of wrecked Christmas roses, nearly over, but still, in the coldest corners, the lovely buds like handfuls of snow. There had been such crowded sumptuous tufts of Christmas roses everywhere in the stream-gullies, during the shadow of winter, that these few remaining flowers were hardly noticeable.

I gathered instead the primroses, that smelled of earth and of the weather. There were no snowdrops. I had found the day before a bank of crocuses, pale, fragile, lilac-coloured flowers with dark veins, pricking up keenly like myriad little lilac-coloured flames among the grass, under the olive trees. And I wanted very much to find the snowdrops hanging in the gloom. But there were not any.

I gathered a handful of primroses, then I climbed suddenly, quickly out of the deep watercourse, anxious to get back to the sunshine before the evening fell. Up above I saw the olive trees in their sunny golden grass, and sunlit grey rocks immensely high up. I was afraid lest the evening would fall whilst I was groping about like an otter in the damp and the darkness, that the day of sunshine would be over.

Soon I was up in the sunshine again, on the turf under the olive trees, reassured. It was the upper world of glowing light, and I was safe again.

All the olives were gathered, and the mills were going night and day, making a great, acrid scent of olive oil in preparation, by the lake. The little stream rattled down. A mule driver 'Hued!' to his mules on the Strada Vecchia. High up, on the Strada Nuova, the beautiful, new, military high-road, which winds with beautiful curves up the mountain-side, crossing the same stream several times in clear-leaping bridges, travelling cut out of sheer slope high above the lake, winding beautifully and gracefully forward to the Austrian frontier, where it ends: high up on the lovely swinging road, in the strong evening sunshine, I saw a bullock wagon moving like a vision, though the clanking of the wagon and the crack of the bullock whip resounded close in my ears.

Everything was clear and sun-coloured up there, clear-grey rocks partaking of the sky, tawny grass and scrub, browny-green spires of cypresses, and then the mist of grey-green olives fuming down to the lake-side. There was no shadow, only clear sun-substance built up to the sky, a bullock wagon moving slowly in the high sunlight, along the uppermost terrace of the military road. I sat in the warm stillness of the transcendent afternoon.

The four o'clock steamer was creeping down the lake from the Austrian end, creeping under the cliffs. Far away, the Verona side, beyond the Island, lay fused in dim gold.

The mountain opposite was so still, that my heart seemed to fade in its beating, as if it too would be still. All was perfectly still, pure substance. The little steamer on the floor of the world below, the mules down the road cast no shadow. They too were pure sun-substance travelling on the surface of the sun-made world.

A cricket hopped near me. Then I remembered that it was Saturday afternoon, when a strange suspension comes over the world. And then, just below me, I saw two monks walking in their garden between the naked, bony vines, walking in their wintry garden of bony vines and olive trees, their brown cassocks passing between the brown vine-stocks, their heads bare to the sunshine, sometimes a glint of light as their feet strode from under their skirts.

It was so still, everything so perfectly suspended, that I felt them talking. They marched with the peculiar march of monks, a long, loping stride, their heads together, their skirts swaying slowly, two brown monks with hidden hands, sliding under the bony vines and beside the cabbages, their heads always together in hidden converse. It was as if I were attending with my dark soul to their inaudible undertone. All the time I sat still in silence, I was one with them, a partaker, though I could hear no sound of their voices. I went with the long stride of their skirted feet, that slid springless and noiseless from end to end of the garden, and back again. Their hands were kept down at their sides, hidden in the long sleeves and

15

the skirts of their robes. They did not touch each other, nor gesticulate as they walked. There was no motion save the long, furtive stride and the heads leaning together. Yet there was an eagerness in their conversation. Almost like shadow-creatures ventured out of their cold, obscure element, they went backwards and forwards in their wintry garden, thinking nobody could see them.

Across, above them, was the faint, rousing dazzle of snow. They never looked up. But the dazzle of snow began to glow as they walked, the wonderful, faint, ethereal flush of the long range of snow in the heavens, at evening, began to kindle. Another world was coming to pass, the cold, rare night. It was dawning in exquisite, icy rose upon the long mountain-summit opposite. The monks walked backwards and forwards, talking, in the first undershadow.

And I noticed that up above the snow, frail in the bluish sky, a frail moon had put forth, like a thin, scalloped film of ice floated out on the slow current of the coming night. And a bell sounded.

And still the monks were pacing backwards and forwards, backwards and forwards, with a strange, neutral regularity.

The shadows were coming across everything, because of the mountains in the West. Already the olive wood where I sat was extinguished. This was the world of the monks, the rim of pallor between night and day. Here they paced, backwards and forwards, backwards and forwards, in the neutral, shadowless light of shadow.

Neither the flare of day nor the completeness of night reached them, they paced the narrow path of the twilight, treading in the neutrality of the law. Neither the blood nor the spirit spoke in them, only the law, the abstraction of the average. The infinite is positive and negative. But the average is only neutral. And the monks trod backward and forward down the line of neutrality.

Meanwhile, on the length of mountain-ridge, the snow grew rosy-incandescent, like heaven breaking into blossom. After all, eternal not-being and eternal being are the same. In the rosy snow that shone in heaven over a darkened earth was the ecstasy of consummation. Night and day are one, light and dark are one, both the same in the origin and in the issue, both the same in the moment of ecstasy, light fused in darkness and darkness fused in light, as in the rosy snow above the twilight.

But in the monks it was not ecstasy, in them it was neutrality, the under earth. Transcendent, above the shadowed, twilit earth was the rosy snow of ecstasy. But spreading far over us, down below, was the neutrality of the twilight, of the monks. The flesh neutralising the spirit, the spirit neutralising the flesh, the law of the average asserted, this was the monks as they paced backward and forward.

The moon climbed higher, away from the snowy, fading

ridge, she became gradually herself. Between the roots of the olive tree was a rosy-tipped daisy just going to sleep. I gathered it and put it among the frail, moony little bunch of primroses, so that its sleep should warm the rest. Also I put in some little periwinkles, that were very blue, reminding me of the eyes of the old woman.

The day was gone, the twilight was gone, and the snow was invisible as I came down to the side of the lake. Only the moon, white and shining, was in the sky, like a woman glorying in her own loveliness as she loiters superbly to the gaze of all the world, looking sometimes through the fringe of dark olive leaves, sometimes looking at her own superb, quivering body, wholly naked in the water of the lake.

My little old woman was gone. She, all day-sunshine, would have none of the moon. Always she must live like a bird, looking down on all the world at once, so that it lay all subsidiary to herself, herself the wakeful consciousness hovering over the world like a hawk, like a sleep of wakefulness. And, like a bird, she went to sleep as the shadows came.

She did not know the yielding up of the senses and the possession of the unknown, through the senses, which happens under a superb moon. The all-glorious sun knows none of these yieldings up. He takes his way. And the daisies at once go to sleep. And the soul of the old spinning-woman also closed up at sunset, the rest was a sleep, a cessation.

It is all so strange and varied: the dark-skinned Italians ecstatic in the night and the moon, the blue-eyed old woman ecstatic in the busy sunshine, the monks in the garden below, who are supposed to unite both, passing only in the neutrality of the average. Where, then, is the meeting-point: where in mankind is the ecstasy of light and dark together, the supreme transcendence of the afterglow, day hovering in the embrace of the coming night like two angels embracing in the heavens, like Eurydice in the arms of Orpheus, or Persephone embraced by Pluto?

Where is the supreme ecstasy in mankind, which makes day a delight and night a delight, purpose an ecstasy and a concourse in ecstasy, and single abandon of the single body and soul also an ecstasy under the moon? Where is the transcendent knowledge in our hearts, uniting sun and darkness, day and night, spirit and senses? Why do we not know that the two in consummation are one; that each is only part; partial and alone for ever; but that the two in consummation are perfect, beyond the range of loneliness or solitude?

Il Duro

The first time I saw Il Duro was on a sunny day when there came up a party of pleasure-makers to San Gaudenzio. They were three women and three men. The women were in cotton frocks, one a large, dark, florid woman in pink, the other two rather insignificant. The men I scarcely noticed at first, except that two were young and one elderly.

They were a queer party, even on a feast day, coming up purely for pleasure, in the morning, strange, and slightly uncertain, advancing between the vines. They greeted Maria and Paolo in loud, coarse voices. There was something blowsy and uncertain and hesitating about the women in particular, which made one at once notice them.

Then a picnic was arranged for them out of doors, on the grass. They sat just in front of the house, under the olive tree, beyond the well. It should have been pretty, the women in their cotton frocks and their friends, sitting with wine and food in the spring sunshine. But somehow it was not: it was hard and slightly ugly.

But since they were picnicking out of doors, we must do so too. We were at once envious. But Maria was a little unwilling, and then she set a table for us.

The strange party did not speak to us, they seemed slightly uneasy and angry at our presence. I asked Maria who they were. She lifted her shoulders, and, after a second's cold pause, said they were people from down below, and then, in her rather strident, shrill, slightly bitter, slightly derogatory voice, she added:

'They are not people for you, Signore. You don't know them.'

She spoke slightly angrily and contemptuously of them, rather protectively of me. So that vaguely I gathered that they were not quite 'respectable.'

Only one man came into the house. He was very handsome, beautiful rather, a man of thirty-two or -three, with a clear golden skin, and perfectly turned face, something godlike. But the expression was strange. His hair was jet black and fine and smooth, glossy as a bird's wing, his brows were beautifully drawn, calm above his grey eyes, that had long, dark lashes.

His eyes, however, had a sinister light in them, a pale, slightly repelling gleam, very much like a god's pale-gleaming eyes, with the same vivid pallor. And all his face had the slightly malignant, suffering look of a satyr. Yet he was very beautiful.

He walked quickly and surely, with his head rather down, passing from his desire to his object, absorbed, yet curiously indifferent, as if the transit were in a strange world, as if none of what he was doing were worth the while. Yet he did it for his own pleasure, and the light on his face, a pale, strange gleam through his clear skin, remained like a translucent smile, unchanging as time.

He seemed familiar with the household, he came and fetched wine at his will. Maria was angry with him. She railed loudly and violently. He was unchanged. He went out with the wine to the party on the grass. Maria regarded them all with some hostility.

They drank a good deal out there in the sunshine. The women and the older man talked floridly. Il Duro crouched at the feast in his curious fashion – he had strangely flexible loins, upon which he seemed to crouch forward. But he was separate, like an animal that remains quite single, no matter where it is.

The party remained until about two o'clock. Then, slightly flushed, it moved on in a ragged group up to the village beyond. I do not know if they went to one of the inns of the stony village, or to the large strange house which belonged to the rich young grocer of the village below, a house kept only for feasts and riots, uninhabited for the most part. Maria would tell me nothing about them. Only the young well-to-do grocer, who had lived in Vienna, the Bertolotti, came later in the afternoon enquiring for the party.

And towards sunset I saw the elderly man of the group stumbling home very drunk down the path, after the two women, who had gone on in front. Then Paolo sent Giovanni to see the drunken one safely past the landslip, which was dangerous. Altogether it was an unsatisfactory business, very much like any other such party in any other country.

Then in the evening Il Duro came in. His name is Faustino, but everybody in the village has a nickname, which is almost invariably used. He came in and asked for supper. We had all eaten. So he ate a little food alone at the table, whilst we sat round the fire.

Afterwards we played 'Up, Jenkins.' That was the one game we played with the peasants, except that exciting one of theirs, which consists in shouting in rapid succession your guesses at the number of fingers rapidly spread out and shut into the hands again upon the table.

Il Duro joined in the game. And that was because he had been in America, and now was rich. He felt he could come near to the strange Signori. But he was always inscrutable.

It was queer to look at the hands spread on the table: the Englishwomen, having rings on their soft fingers; the large fresh hands of the elder boy, the brown paws of the younger; Paolo's distorted great hard hands of a peasant; and the big, dark brown, animal, shapely hands of Faustino.

He had been in America first for two years and then for five years – seven years altogether – but he only spoke a very little English. He was always with Italians. He had

23

served chiefly in a flag factory, and had had very little to
do save to push a trolley with flags from the dyeing-room
to the drying-room – I believe it was this.

Then he had come home from America with a fair
amount of money, he had taken his uncle's garden, had
inherited his uncle's little house, and he lived quite alone.

He was rich, Maria said, shouting in her strident voice.
He at once disclaimed it, peasant-wise. But before the
Signori he was glad also to appear rich. He was mean,
that was more, Maria cried, half-teasing, half getting
at him.

He attended to his garden, grew vegetables all the year
round, lived in his little house, and in spring made good
money as a vine-grafter: he was an expert vine-grafter.

After the boys had gone to bed he sat and talked to me.
He was curiously attractive and curiously beautiful, but
somehow like stone in his clear colouring and his clear-cut
face. His temples, with the black hair, were distinct and
fine as a work of art.

But always his eyes had this strange, half-diabolic,
half-tortured pale gleam, like a goat's, and his mouth was
shut almost uglily, his cheeks stern. His moustache was
brown, his teeth strong and spaced. The women said it
was a pity his moustache was brown.

'Peccato! – sa, per bellezza, i baffi neri – ah-h!'

Then a long-drawn exclamation of voluptuous
appreciation.

'You live quite alone?' I said to him.

He did. And even when he had been ill he was alone. He had been ill two years before. His cheeks seemed to harden like marble, and to become pale at the thought. He was afraid, like marble with fear.

'But why?' I said, 'why do you live alone? You are sad – è triste.'

He looked at me with his queer, pale eyes.

I felt a great static misery in him, something very strange.

'Triste!' he repeated, stiffening up, hostile. I could not understand.

'Vuol' dire che hai l'aria dolorosa,' cried Maria, like a chorus interpreting. And there was always a sort of loud ring of challenge somewhere in her voice.

'Sad,' I said, in English.

'Sad!' he repeated, also in English. And he did not smile or change, only his face seemed to become more stone-like. And he only looked at me, into my eyes, with the long, pale, steady, inscrutable look of a goat, I can only repeat, something stone-like.

'Why,' I said, 'don't you marry? Man doesn't live alone.'

'I don't marry,' he said to me, in his emphatic, deliberate, cold fashion, 'because I've seen too much. Ho visto troppo.'

'I don't understand,' I said.

Yet I could feel that Paolo, sitting silent, like a monolith also, in the chimney opening, he understood: Maria also understood.

Il Duro looked again steadily into my eyes.

'Ho visto troppo,' he repeated, and the words seemed engraved on stone. 'I've seen too much.'

'But you can marry,' I said, 'however much you have seen, if you have seen all the world.'

He watched me steadily, like a strange creature looking at me.

'What woman?' he said to me.

'You can find a woman – there are plenty of women,' I said.

'Not for me,' he said. 'I have known too many. I've known too much, I can marry nobody.'

'Do you dislike women?' I said.

'No – quite otherwise. I don't think ill of them.'

'Then why can't you marry? Why must you live alone?'

'Why live with a woman?' he said to me, and he looked mockingly. 'Which woman is it to be?'

'You can find her,' I said. 'There are many women.'

Again he shook his head in the stony, final fashion.

'Not for me. I have known too much.'

'But does that prevent you from marrying?'

He looked at me steadily, finally. And I could see it was impossible for us to understand each other, or for me to understand him. I could not understand the strange white gleam of his eyes, where it came from.

Also I knew he liked me very much, almost loved me, which again was strange and puzzling. It was as if he were

a fairy, a faun, and had no soul. But he gave me a feeling
of vivid sadness, a sadness that gleamed like phosphores-
cence. He himself was not sad. There was a completeness
about him, about the pallid otherworld he inhabited,
which excluded sadness. It was too complete, too final,
too defined. There was no yearning, no vague merging
off into mistiness . . . He was as clear and fine as
semi-transparent rock, as a substance in moonlight. He
seemed like a crystal that has achieved its final shape and
has nothing more to achieve.

That night he slept on the floor of the sitting-room. In
the morning he was gone. But a week after he came again,
to graft the vines.

All the morning and the afternoon he was among the
vines, crouching before them, cutting them back with his
sharp, bright knife, amazingly swift and sure, like a god.
It filled me with a sort of panic to see him crouched flex-
ibly, like some strange animal god, doubled on his
haunches, before the young vines, and swiftly, vividly,
without thought, cut, cut, cut at the young budding
shoots, which fell unheeded on to the earth. Then again
he strode with his curious, half goat-like movement across
the garden, to prepare the lime.

He mixed the messy stuff, cow-dung and lime and water
and earth, carefully with his hands, as if he understood
that too. He was not a worker. He was a creature in intim-
ate communion with the sensible world, knowing purely
by touch the limey mess he mixed amongst, knowing as

if by relation between that soft matter and the matter of himself.

Then again he strode over the earth, a gleaming piece of earth himself, moving to the young vines. Quickly, with a few clean cuts of the knife, he prepared the new shoot, which he had picked out of a handful which lay beside him on the ground, he went finely to the quick of the plant, inserted the graft, then bound it up, fast, hard.

It was like God grafting the life of man upon the body of the earth, intimately, conjuring with his own flesh.

All the while Paolo stood by, somehow excluded from the mystery, talking to me, to Faustino. And Il Duro answered easily, as if his mind were disengaged. It was his senses that were absorbed in the sensible life of the plant and the lime and the cow-dung he handled.

Watching him, watching his absorbed, bestial, and yet god-like crouching before the plant, as if he were the god of lower life, I somehow understood his isolation, why he did not marry. Pan and the ministers of Pan do not marry, the sylvan gods. They are single and isolated in their being.

It is in the spirit that marriage takes place. In the flesh there is connection; but only in the spirit is there a new thing created out of two different antithetic things. In the body I am conjoined with the woman. But in the spirit my conjunction with her creates a third thing, an absolute, a Word, which is neither me nor her, nor of me nor of her, but which is absolute.

And Faustino had none of this spirit. In him sensation itself was absolute – not spiritual consummation, but physical sensation. So he could not marry, it was not for him. He belonged to the god Pan, to the absolute of the senses.

All the while his beauty, so perfect and so defined, fascinated me, a strange static perfection about him. But his movements, whilst they fascinated, also repelled. I can always see him crouched before the vines on his haunches, his haunches doubled together in a complete animal unconsciousness, his face seeming in its strange golden pallor and its hardness of line, with the gleaming black of the fine hair on the brow and temples, like something reflective, like the reflecting surface of a stone that gleams out of the depths of night. It was like darkness revealed in its steady, unchanging pallor.

Again he stayed through the evening, having quarrelled once more with the Maria about money. He quarrelled violently, yet coldly. There was something terrifying in it. And as soon as the matter of dispute was settled, all trace of interest or feeling vanished from him.

Yet he liked, above all things, to be near the English Signori. They seemed to exercise a sort of magnetic attraction over him. It was something of the purely physical world, as a magnetised needle swings towards soft iron. He was quite helpless in the relation. Only by mechanical attraction he gravitated into line with us.

But there was nothing between us except our complete difference. It was like night and day flowing together.

John

Besides Il Duro, we found another Italian who could speak English, this time quite well. We had walked about four or five miles up the lake, getting higher and higher. Then quite suddenly, on the shoulder of a bluff far up, we came on a village, icy cold, and as if forgotten.

We went into the inn to drink something hot. The fire of olive sticks was burning in the open chimney, one or two men were talking at a table, a young woman with a baby stood by the fire watching something boil in a large pot. Another woman was seen in the house-place beyond.

In the chimney-seats sat a young mule-driver, who had left his two mules at the door of the inn, and opposite him an elderly stout man. They got down and offered us the seats of honour, which we accepted with due courtesy.

The chimneys are like the wide open chimney-places of old English cottages, but the hearth is raised about a foot and a half or two feet from the floor, so that the fire is almost level with the hands, and those who sit in the chimney-seats are raised above the audience in the room, something like two gods flanking the fire, looking out of the cave of ruddy darkness into the open, lower world of the room.

We asked for coffee with milk and rum. The stout landlord took a seat near us below. The comely young woman with the baby took the tin coffee-pot that stood among the grey ashes, put in fresh coffee among the old bottoms, filled it with water, then pushed it more into the fire.

The landlord turned to us with the usual naïve, curious deference, and the usual question:

'You are Germans?'

'English.'

'Ah – Inglesi.'

Then there is a new note of cordiality – or so I always imagine – and the rather rough, cattle-like men who are sitting with their wine round the table look up more amicably. They do not like being intruded upon. Only the landlord is always affable.

'I have a son who speaks English,' he says: he is a handsome, courtly old man, of the Falstaff sort.

'Oh!'

'He has been in America.'

'And where is he now?'

'He is at home. O – Nicoletta, where is the Giovann'?'

The comely young woman with the baby came in.

'He is with the band,' she said.

The old landlord looked at her with pride.

'This is my daughter-in-law,' he said.

She smiled readily to the Signora.

'And the baby?' we asked.

'Mio figlio,' cried the young woman, in the strong, penetrating voice of these women. And she came forward to show the child to the Signora.

It was a bonny baby: the whole company was united in adoration and service of the bambino. There was a moment of suspension, when religious submission seemed to come over the inn-room.

Then the Signora began to talk, and it broke upon the Italian child-reverence.

'What is he called?'

'Oscare,' came the ringing note of pride. And the mother talked to the baby in dialect. All, men and women alike, felt themselves glorified by the presence of the child.

At last the coffee in the tin coffee-pot was boiling and frothing out of spout and lid. The milk in the little copper pan was also hot, among the ashes. So we had our drink at last.

The landlord was anxious for us to see Giovanni, his son. There was a village band performing up the street, in front of the house of a colonel who had come home wounded from Tripoli. Everybody in the village was wildly proud about the colonel and about the brass band, the music of which was execrable.

We just looked into the street. The band of uncouth fellows was playing the same tune over and over again before a desolate, newish house. A crowd of desolate, forgotten villagers stood round, in the cold upper air. It seemed altogether that the place was forgotten by God and man.

But the landlord, burly, courteous, handsome, pointed out with a flourish the Giovanni, standing in the band playing a cornet. The band itself consisted only of five men, rather like beggars in the street. But Giovanni was the strangest! He was tall and thin and somewhat German-looking, wearing shabby American clothes and a very high double collar and a small American crush hat. He looked entirely like a ne'er-do-well who plays a violin in the street, dressed in the most down-at-heel, sordid respectability.

'That is he – you see, Signore – the young one under the balcony.'

The father spoke with love and pride, and the father was a gentleman, like Falstaff, a pure gentleman. The daughter-in-law also peered out to look at Il Giovann', who was evidently a figure of repute, in his sordid, degenerate American respectability. Meanwhile, this figure of repute blew himself red in the face, producing staccato strains on his cornet. And the crowd stood desolate and forsaken in the cold, upper afternoon.

Then there was a sudden rugged 'Evviva, Evviva!' from the people, the band stopped playing, somebody valiantly broke into a line of the song:

> Tripoli, sarà italiana,
> Sarà italiana al rombo del cannon'.

The colonel had appeared on the balcony, a smallish man, very yellow in the face, with grizzled black hair and very shabby legs. They all seemed so sordidly, hopelessly shabby.

He suddenly began to speak, leaning forward, hot and feverish and yellow, upon the iron rail of the balcony. There was something hot and marshy and sick about him, slightly repulsive, less than human. He told his fellow-villagers how he loved them, how, when he lay uncovered on the sands of Tripoli, week after week, he had known they were watching him from the Alpine height of the village, he could feel that where he was they were all looking. When the Arabs came rushing like things gone mad, and he had received his wound, he had known that in his own village, among his own dear ones, there was recovery. Love would heal the wounds, the home country was a lover who would heal all her sons' wounds with love.

Among the grey, desolate crowd were sharp, rending 'Bravos!' – the people were in tears – the landlord at my side was repeating softly, abstractedly: 'Caro – caro – Ettore, caro colonello—' and when it was finished, and the little colonel with shabby, humiliated legs was gone in, he turned to me, and said, with challenge that almost frightened me:

'Un brav' uomo.'

'Bravissimo,' I said.

Then we, too, went indoors.

It was all, somehow, grey and hopeless and acrid, unendurable.

The colonel, poor devil – we knew him afterwards – is now dead. It is strange that he is dead. There is something repulsive to me in the thought of his lying dead: such a humiliating, somehow degraded corpse. Death has no beauty in Italy, unless it be violent. The death of man or woman through sickness is an occasion of horror, repulsive. They belong entirely to life, they are so limited to life, these people.

Soon the Giovanni came home, and took his cornet upstairs. Then he came to see us. He was an ingenuous youth, sordidly shabby and dirty. His fair hair was long and uneven, his very high starched collar made one aware that his neck and his ears were not clean, his American crimson tie was ugly, his clothes looked as if they had been kicking about on the floor for a year.

Yet his blue eyes were warm and his manner and speech very gentle.

'You will speak English with us,' I said.

'Oh,' he said, smiling and shaking his head, 'I could speak English very well. But it is two years that I don't speak it now, over two years now, so I don't speak it.'

'But you speak it very well.'

'No. It is two years that I have not spoke, not a word – so, you see, I have –'

'You have forgotten it? No, you haven't. It will quickly come back.'

'If I hear it – when I go to America – then I shall – I
shall –'

'You will soon pick it up.'

'Yes – I shall pick it up.'

The landlord, who had been watching with pride, now
went away. The wife also went away, and we were left with
the shy, gentle, dirty, and frowsily-dressed Giovanni.

He laughed in his sensitive, quick fashion.

'The women in America, when they came into the store,
they said, "Where is John, where is John?" Yes, they
liked me.'

And he laughed again, glancing with vague, warm,
blue eyes, very shy, very coiled upon himself with
sensitiveness.

He had managed a store in America, in a smallish town.
I glanced at his reddish, smooth, rather knuckly hands,
and thin wrists in the frayed cuff. They were real shop-
man's hands.

The landlord brought some special feast-day cake, so
overjoyed he was to have his Giovanni speaking English
with the Signoria.

When we went away, we asked 'John' to come down to
our villa to see us. We scarcely expected him to turn up.

Yet one morning he appeared, at about half-past nine,
just as we were finishing breakfast. It was sunny and warm
and beautiful, so we asked him please to come with us
picnicking.

He was a queer shoot, again, in his unkempt longish

hair and slovenly clothes, a sort of very vulgar down-at-heel American in appearance. And he was transported with shyness. Yet ours was the world he had chosen as his own, so he took his place bravely and simply, a hanger-on.

We climbed up the water-course in the mountain-side, up to a smooth little lawn under the olive trees, where daisies were flowering and gladioli were in bud. It was a tiny little lawn of grass in a level crevice, and sitting there we had the world below us, the lake, the distant island, the far-off, low Verona shore.

Then 'John' began to talk, and he talked continuously, like a foreigner, not saying the things he would have said in Italian, but following the suggestion and scope of his limited English.

In the first place, he loved his father – it was 'my father, my father' always. His father had a little shop as well as the inn in the village above. So John had had some education. He had been sent to Brescia and then to Verona to school, and there had taken his examinations to become a civil engineer. He was clever, and could pass his examinations. But he never finished his course. His mother died, and his father, disconsolate, had wanted him at home. Then he had gone back, when he was sixteen or seventeen, to the village beyond the lake, to be with his father and to look after the shop.

'But didn't you mind giving up all your work?' I said.

He did not quite understand.

'My father wanted me to come back,' he said.

It was evident that Giovanni had had no definite conception of what he was doing or what he wanted to do. His father, wishing to make a gentleman of him, had sent him to school in Verona. By accident he had been moved on into the engineering course. When it all fizzled to an end, and he returned half-baked to the remote, desolate village of the mountain-side, he was not disappointed or chagrined. He had never conceived of a coherent purposive life. Either one stayed in the village, like a lodged stone, or one made random excursions into the world, across the world. It was all aimless and purposeless.

So he had stayed a while with his father, then he had gone, just as aimlessly, with a party of men who were emigrating to America. He had taken some money, had drifted about, living in the most comfortless, wretched fashion, then he had found a place somewhere in Pennsylvania, in a dry goods store. This was when he was seventeen or eighteen years old.

All this seemed to have happened to him without his being very much affected, at least consciously. His nature was simple and self-complete. Yet not so self-complete as that of Il Duro or Paolo. They had passed through the foreign world and been quite untouched. Their souls were static, it was the world that had flowed unstable by.

But John was more sensitive, he had come more into contact with his new surroundings. He had attended night classes almost every evening, and had been taught English like a child. He had loved the American free school, the teachers, the work.

But he had suffered very much in America. With his curious, over-sensitive, wincing laugh, he told us how the boys had followed him and jeered at him, calling after him, 'You damn Dago, you damn Dago.' They had stopped him and his friend in the street and taken away their hats, and spat into them, and made water into them. So that at last he had gone mad. They were youths and men who always tortured him, using bad language which startled us very much as he repeated it, there on the little lawn under the olive trees, above the perfect lake: English obscenities and abuse so coarse and startling that we bit our lips, shocked almost into laughter, whilst John, simple and natural, and somehow, for all his long hair and dirty appearance, flower-like in soul, repeated to us these things which may never be repeated in decent company.

'Oh,' he said, 'at last, I get mad. When they come one day, shouting, "You damn Dago, dirty dog," and will take my hat again, oh, I get mad, and I would kill them. I would kill them, I am so mad. I run to them, and throw one to the floor, and I tread on him while I go upon another, the biggest. Though they hit me and kick me all over, I feel nothing, I am mad. I throw the biggest to the floor, a man, he is older than I am, and I hit him, so hard I would kill him. When the others see it they are afraid, they throw stones and hit me on the face. But I don't feel it – I don't know nothing. I hit the man on the floor, I almost kill him. I forget everything except I will kill him –'

'But you didn't?'

'No – I don't know –' and he laughed his queer, shaken laugh. 'The other man, what was with me, my friend, he came to me and we went away. Oh, I was mad, I completely mad. I would have killed them.'

He was trembling slightly, and his eyes were dilated with a strange, greyish-blue fire that was very painful and elemental. He looked beside himself. But he was by no means mad.

We were shaken by the vivid, lambent excitement of the youth, we wished him to forget. We were shocked, too, in our souls to see the pure elemental flame shaken out of his gentle, sensitive nature. By his slight, crinkled laugh we could see how much he had suffered. He had gone out and faced the world, and he had kept his place, stranger and Dago though he was.

'They never came after me no more, not all the while I was there.'

Then he said he became the foreman in the store – at first he was only assistant. It was the best store in the town, and many English ladies came, and some Germans. He liked the English ladies very much: they always wanted him to be in the store. He wore white clothes there, and they would say:

'You look very nice in the white coat, John,' or else:

'Let John come, he can find it,' or else they said:

'John speaks like a born American.'

This pleased him very much.

In the end, he said, he earned a hundred dollars a month. He lived with the extraordinary frugality of the Italians, and had quite a lot of money.

He was not like Il Duro. Faustino had lived in a state of miserliness almost in America, but then he had had his debauches of shows and wine and carousals. John went chiefly to the schools, in one of which he was even asked to teach Italian. His knowledge of his own language was remarkable and most unusual!

'But what,' I asked, 'brought you back?'

'It was my father. You see, if I did not come to have my military service, I must stay till I am forty. So I think perhaps my father will be dead, I shall never see him. So I came.'

He had come home when he was twenty to fulfil his military duties. At home he had married. He was very fond of his wife, but he had no conception of love in the old sense. His wife was like the past, to which he was wedded. Out of her he begot his child, as out of the past. But the future was all beyond her, apart from her. He was going away again, now, to America. He had been some nine months at home after his military service was over. He had no more to do. Now he was leaving his wife and child and his father to go to America.

'But why,' I said, 'Why? You are not poor, you can manage the shop in your village.'

'Yes,' he said. 'But I will go to America. Perhaps I shall go into the store again, the same.'

'But is it not just the same as managing the shop at home?'

'No – no – it is quite different.'

Then he told us how he bought goods in Brescia and in Salò for the shop at home, how he had rigged up a funicular with the assistance of the village, an overhead wire by which you could haul the goods up the face of the cliffs right high up, to within a mile of the village. He was very proud of this. And sometimes he himself went down the funicular to the water's edge, to the boat, when he was in a hurry. This also pleased him.

But he was going to Brescia this day to see about going again to America. Perhaps in another month he would be gone.

It was a great puzzle to me why he would go. He could not say himself. He would stay four or five years, then he would come home again to see his father – and his wife and child.

There was a strange, almost frightening destiny upon him, which seemed to take him away, always away from home, from the past, to that great, raw America. He seemed scarcely like a person with individual choice, more like a creature under the influence of fate which was

disintegrating the old life and precipitating him, a fragment inconclusive, into the new chaos.

He submitted to it all with a perfect unquestioning
simplicity, never even knowing that he suffered, that he
must suffer disintegration from the old life. He was moved
entirely from within, he never questioned his inevitable
impulse.

'They say to me, "Don't go – don't go" –' he shook his
head. 'But I say I will go.'

And at that it was finished.

So we saw him off at the little quay, going down the
lake. He would return at evening, and be pulled up in his
funicular basket. And in a month's time he would be
standing on the same lake steamer going to America.

Nothing was more painful than to see him standing
there in his degraded, sordid American clothes, on the
deck of the steamer, waving us good-bye, belonging in
his final desire to our world, the world of consciousness
and deliberate action. With his candid, open, unquestioning face, he seemed like a prisoner being conveyed from
one form of life to another, or like a soul in trajectory,
that has not yet found a resting-place.

What were wife and child to him: they were the last
steps of the past. His father was the continent behind
him; his wife and child the foreshore of the past; but his
face was set outwards, away from it all – whither, neither
he nor anybody knew, but he called it America.

*

When I was in Constance the weather was misty and ener-
vating and depressing, it was no pleasure to travel on the
big, flat, desolate lake.

When I went from Constance, it was on a small steamer
down the Rhine to Schaffhausen. That was beautiful.
Still, the mist hung over the waters, over the wide shal-
lows of the river, and the sun, coming through the
morning, made lovely yellow lights beneath the bluish
haze, so that it seemed like the beginning of the world.
And there was a hawk in the upper air fighting with two
crows, or two rooks. Ever they rose higher and higher,
the crow flickering above the attacking hawk, the fight
going on like some strange symbol in the sky, the Germans on deck watching with pleasure.

Then we passed out of sight, between wooded banks
and under bridges where quaint villages of old romance
piled their red and coloured pointed roofs beside the
water, very still, remote, lost in the vagueness of the past.
It could not be that they were real. Even when the boat
put in to shore, and the customs officials came to look,
the village remained remote in the romantic past of High
Germany, the Germany of fairy tales and minstrels and
craftsmen. The poignancy of the past was almost unbear-
able, floating there in colour upon the haze of the river.

We went by some swimmers, whose white, shadowy
bodies trembled near the side of the steamer, under water.
One man with a round, fair head, lifted his face and one
arm from the water and shouted a greeting to us, as if he

were a Niebelung, saluting with bright arm lifted from the water, his face laughing, the fair moustache hanging over his mouth. Then his white body swirled in the water, and he was gone, swimming with the side stroke.

Schaffhausen the town, half old and bygone, half modern, with breweries and industries, that is not very real. Schaffhausen Falls, with their factory in the midst and their hotel at the bottom, and the general cinematograph effect, they are ugly.

It was afternoon when I set out to walk from the Falls to Italy, across Switzerland. I remember the big, fat, rather gloomy fields of this part of Baden, damp and unliving. I remember I found some apples under a tree in a field near a railway embankment, then some mushrooms, and I ate both. Then I came on to a long, desolate high road, with dreary, withered trees on either side, and flanked by great fields where groups of men and women were working. They looked at me as I went by down the long, long road, alone and exposed and out of the world.

I remember nobody came at the border village to examine my pack, I passed through unchallenged. All was quiet and lifeless and hopeless, with big stretches of heavy land.

Till sunset came, very red and purple, and suddenly, from the heavy spacious open land I dropped sharply into the Rhine valley again, suddenly, as if into another glamorous world.

There was the river rushing along between its high,

45

mysterious, romantic banks, which were high as hills, and covered with vine. And there was the village of tall, quaint houses flickering its lights on to the deep-flowing river, and quite silent, save for the rushing of water.

There was a fine covered bridge, very dark. I went to the middle, and looked through the opening at the dark water below, at the façade of square lights, the tall village-front towering remote and silent above the river. The hill rose on either side the flood, down here was a small, forgotten, wonderful world, that belonged to the date of isolated village communities and wandering minstrels.

So I went back to the inn of 'The Golden Stag,' and, climbing some steps, I made a loud noise. A woman came, and I asked for food. She led me through a room where were enormous barrels, ten feet in diameter, lying fatly on their sides; then through a large stone-clean kitchen, with bright pans, ancient as the Meistersinger; then up some steps and into the long guest-room, where a few tables were laid for supper.

A few people were eating. I asked for Abendessen, and sat by the window looking at the darkness of the river below, the covered bridge, the dark hill opposite, crested with its few lights.

Then I ate a very large quantity of knoedel soup, and bread, and drank beer, and was very sleepy. Only one or two village men came in, and these soon went again, the place was dead still. Only at a long table on the opposite side of the room were seated seven or eight men, ragged, disreputable, some impudent – another came in late – the landlady gave them all thick soup with dumplings and bread and meat, serving them in a sort of brief disapprobation. They sat at the long table, eight or nine tramps and beggars and wanderers out of work, and they ate with a sort of cheerful callousness and brutality for the most part, and as if ravenously, looking round and grinning sometimes, subdued, cowed, like prisoners, and yet impudent. At the end one shouted to know where he was to sleep. The landlady called to the young serving-woman, and in a classic German severity of disapprobation, they were led up the stone stairs to their room. They tramped off in threes and twos, making a bad, mean, humiliated exit. It was not yet eight o'clock. The landlady sat talking to one bearded man, staid and severe, whilst, with her work on the table, she sewed steadily.

As the beggars and wanderers went slinking out of the room, some called impudently, cheerfully:

'Nacht, Frau Wirtin – G'Nacht, Wirtin –'te Nacht, Frau,' to all of which the hostess answered a stereotyped 'Gute Nacht,' never turning her head from her sewing or indicating by the faintest movement that she was addressing the men who were filing raggedly to the doorway.

So the room was empty, save for the landlady and her sewing, the staid, elderly villager to whom she was talking in the unbeautiful dialect, and the young serving-woman who was clearing away the plates and basins of the tramps and beggars.

Then the villager also went.

'Gute Nacht, Frau Seidl,' to the landlady; 'Gute Nacht,' at random, to me.

So I looked at the newspaper. Then I asked the landlady for a cigarette, not knowing how else to begin. So she came to my table, and we talked.

It pleased me to take upon myself a sort of romantic, wandering character; she said my German was 'schön'; a little goes a long way.

So I asked her who were the men who had sat at the long table. She became rather stiff and curt.

'They are the men looking for work,' she said, as if the subject were disagreeable.

'But why do they come here, so many?' I asked.

Then she told me that they were going out of the country: this was almost the last village of the border: that the relieving officer in each village was empowered to give to every vagrant a ticket entitling the holder to an evening meal, bed, and bread in the morning, at a certain inn. This was the inn for the vagrants coming to this village. The landlady received fourpence per head, I believe it was, for each of these wanderers.

'Little enough,' I said.

'Nothing,' she replied.

She did not like the subject at all. Only her respect for me made her answer.

The Florence Museum

It would perhaps be easier to go to the Archaeological Museum in Florence, to look at the etruscan collection, if we decided once and for all that there never were any Etruscans. Because, in the cut-and-dried museum sense, there never were.

The Etruscans were not a race, that is obvious. And they were not a nation. They were not even as much of a people as the Romans of the Augustan age were: and a Roman of the Augustan age might be a Latin, an Etruscan, a Sabine, a Samnite, an Umbrian, a Celt, a Greek, a Jew, or almost anything else of the world of that day. He might come from any tribe or race, almost, and still be first and foremost a Roman. 'I am a Roman.'

What makes a civilised people is not blood, but some dominant culture-principle. Certain blood-streams give rise to, or are sympathetic to, certain culture principles. The handful of original Romans in Latium contained the germ of the civilising principle of Rome, that was all.

But there was not even an original handful of original Etruscans. In Etruria there is no starting-point. Just as there is no starting-point for England, once we have the courage to look beyond Julius Caesar and 55 BC Britain was active and awake and alive long before Caesar saw it. Nor was it a country of blue-painted savages in bear-skins. It had an old culture of its own, older than the little hill of Romulus.

But then the historical invasions started. Romans, Jutes, Angles, Saxons, Danes, Normans, Jews, French: after all, what is England? What does the word England mean, even? What clue would it give to the rise of the English, should all our history be lost? About as good a clue as Tusci or Tyrrheni give to the make-up of the Etruscan.

Etruria is a parallel case to England. In the dim British days before Julius Caesar, there were dim Italian days too, and endless restless Italian tribes and peoples with their own speech and customs and religious practices. They were not just brutes, nor cave-men, because they lived in the days before Homer. They were men, alive and alert, having their own complex forms of expression.

And in those dim days where history does not exist – not because men, intelligent men did not then exist, but because one culture wipes out another as completely as possible; in those dim days, there were invasions, invasion after invasion no doubt, from the wild north on foot, from the old, cultured Aegean basin, in ships. Men kept on coming, and kept on coming: strangers.

But there were two deep emotions or culture-rhythms

which persisted in all the confusion: and one was some old, old Italian rhythm of life, belonging to the soil, which invaded every invader; and the other was the old cosmic consciousness, or culture principle, of the prehistoric Mediterranean, particularly of the eastern Mediterranean. Man is *always* trying to be conscious of the cosmos, the cosmos of life and passion and feeling, desire and death and despair, as well as of physical phenomena. And there are still millions of undreamed-of ways of becoming aware of the cosmos. Which is to say, there are millions of worlds, whole cosmic worlds, to us yet unborn.

Every religion, every philosophy, and science itself, each has a clue to the cosmos, to the becoming aware of the cosmos. Each clue leads to its own goal of consciousness, then is exhausted. So religions exhaust themselves, so science exhausts itself, once the human consciousness reaches its own limit. The infinite of the human consciousness lies in an infinite number of different starts to an infinite number of different goals; which somehow, we know when we get there, is one goal. But the new start is from a point in the hitherto unknown.

What we have to realise in looking at etruscan things is that they reveal the last glimpses of a human cosmic consciousness – or human attempt at cosmic consciousness – different from our own. The idea that our history emerged out of caves and savage lake-dwellings is puerile. Our history emerges out of the closing of a previous great phase of human history, a phase as great as our own. It is much more likely the monkey is descended from us, than we from the monkey.

What we see, in the etruscan remains, is the fag end of the revelation of another form of cosmic consciousness: and also, that salt of the earth, the revelation of the human existence of people who lived and who *were*, in a way somewhat different from our way of living and being. There are two separate things: the artistic or impulsive or culture-expression, and the religious or scientific or civilisation expression of a group of people. The first is based on emotion; the second on concepts.

The Etruscans consisted of all sorts of tribes and distinct peoples: that is obvious: and they did not intermingle. Velathri (Volterra) and Tarquinii were two quite distinct peoples, racially. No doubt they spoke different languages, vulgarly. The thing they had in common was the remains of an old cosmic consciousness, an old religion, an old attempt on man's part to understand, or at least to interpret to himself, the cosmos as he knew it. That was the civilising principle.

Civilisations rise in waves, and pass away in waves. And not till science, or art, tries to catch the ultimate meaning of the symbols that float on the last waves of the prehistoric period; that is, the period before our own; shall we be able to get ourselves into right relation with man as man is and has been and will always be.

In the days before Homer, men in Europe were *not* mere brutes and savages and prognathous monsters: neither were they simple-minded children. Men are always men, and though intelligence takes different forms, men are always intelligent: they are not empty brutes, or dumb-bells *en masse*.

The symbols that come down to us on the last waves of prehistoric culture are the remnants of a vast old attempt made by humanity to form a conception of the universe. The conception was shattered and diminished even by the time it rose to new life, in Egypt. It rose up again, in ancient China and India, in Babylonia and in Asia Minor, in the Druid, in the Teuton, in the Aztec and in the Maya of America, in the very negroes. But each time it rose in a smaller, dying wave, as one tide of consciousness slowly changed to another tide, full of cross-currents. Now our own tide of consciousness is on the ebb, so we can catch the ripples of the tide that ebbed as we arose, and we may read their meaning.

There is no unified and homogeneous etruscan people. There is no Etruscan, pure and simple, and never was: any more than, today, there is one absolute American. There are etruscan characteristics, that is all.

And the real *etruscan* characteristics are the religious symbols. As far as *art* goes, there is no etruscan art. It is an art of all sorts, dominated by an old religious idea.

The religious idea came presumably from the Aegean, the ancient eastern Mediterranean. It was an ebb from an old wider consciousness. If we look at our world today, as far as *culture* goes, it has one culture: the christian-scientific. Whether it be Pekin or Dahomey or New York or Paris, it is more or less the same conception of life and the cosmos, nowadays.

And so it must have been before. The pyramid builders of America must have had some old idea, remnant of an idea, in common with the Egyptian and the Etruscan. And the Celt, the Gaul, the Druid, must have had some lingering idea of the ancient cosmic meaning of the waters, of the leaping fish, of the undying, ever re-born dead, shadowily sharing it with the ancient Italic peoples, as well as with the Hittites or the Lydians.

There are no Etruscans out-and-out, and there never were any. There were different prehistoric tribes stimulated by contact with different peoples from the eastern Mediterranean, and lifted on the last wave of a dying conception of the living cosmos.

That is what one feels. If it is wrong it is wrong. But few things, *that are felt*, are either absolutely wrong or absolutely right. Things absolutely wrong are not felt, they do not arise from contact. They arise from prejudice and pre-conceived notions. As for things absolutely right, they too cannot be felt. Whatever can be felt is capable of many different forms of expression, forms often contradictory, as far as logic or reason goes.

But in the bewildering experience of searching for the Etruscans there is the one steady clue that we can follow:

or rather, there are two clues. The first is the peculiar physical or *bodily*, lively quality of all the art. And this, I take it, is Italian, the result of the Italian soil itself. The Romans got a great deal of their power from *resisting* this curious Italian physical expressiveness: and for the same reason, in the Roman the salt soon lost its savour, in the true Etruscan, never.

The second clue is the more concrete, because more ideal presence of the symbols. Symbols are at least *half* ideas: and so they are half fixed. Emotion and the robust physical gesture are always fluid and changing, never fixed.

So we have the two clues, that of the dominant idea, or half-idea, in the religious symbols; and that of the dominant *feeling*, in the peculiar physical freeness and exuberance and spontaneity. It is the spontaneity of the flesh itself.

These are the two clues to the Etruscan. And they lead from beginning to end, from the point where the Etruscan emerges out of the Oriental, Lydian or Hittite or whatever he may be, till the last days when he is swamped by the Roman and the Greek.